YOUR KNOWLEDGE HAS VALUE

AF145600

- We will publish your bachelor's and master's thesis, essays and papers

- Your own eBook and book - sold worldwide in all relevant shops

- Earn money with each sale

Upload your text at www.GRIN.com and publish for free

Imprint:

Copyright © 2015 GRIN Verlag
Print and binding: Books on Demand GmbH, Norderstedt Germany
ISBN: 9783668753952

Martin Pruschkowski

Entrepreneurship. New Ways of Founding a Startup

Research Proposal for a Master Thesis

GRIN Verlag

GRIN - Your knowledge has value

Since its foundation in 1998, GRIN has specialized in publishing academic texts by students, college teachers and other academics as e-book and printed book. The website www.grin.com is an ideal platform for presenting term papers, final papers, scientific essays, dissertations and specialist books.

Visit us on the internet:

http://www.grin.com/

http://www.facebook.com/grincom

http://www.twitter.com/grin_com

ENTREPRENEURSHIP
NEW WAYS OF FOUNDING A STARTUP

- RESEARCH PROPOSAL FOR THE MASTER THESIS -

Location: Nuremberg

Study program: Master of Business Administration (MBA)

Module: Research Methods

Author: Martin Pruschkowski

4th Academic Semester 2015

Nuremberg, 31 August 2015

Table of Contents

List of Abbreviations

DSM   Deutscher Startup Monitor

KfW   Kreditanstalt für Wiederaufbau

List of Figures

List of Tables

1 Introduction

Each year numerous founders dare with their business ideas the way to independence. For that they found startups. These new small businesses stand for an atmosphere of departure, innovation and growth. Also each business foundation is associated to uncertainties and risks. Nevertheless, according to recent data from the KFW Bank approximately 915,000 people have taken the risk in 2014 just in Germany. That's 47,000 people more than in 2013. The German economy benefits from strong startup activities, because these startups and innovative company founders representing the middle class of the future. They are essential for a sustainable economic development for Germany. These young, not yet established companies play a critical role in expanding an economy because they are challenging the already established players and putting them constant under pressure to increase efficiency potential. Furthermore, the new ideas of the entrepreneurs contribute to the technology renewal of a country and thereby to the improvement in the competitiveness of Germany.[1] Besides that, startups are important drivers for the job market. In 2013 approximately 419,000 equivalent full-time jobs were created by new companies.[2] All this leads to more added value, growth and prosperity. Therefore it could be argued startups are the engines of the economy. For this reason, economies try to create a founder-friendly climate by improving the legal, economic, political, social and cultural conditions for entrepreneurs. According to the German Startup Monitor 2014 founder in Germany evaluate the conditions with unsufficient.[3] Even in an international comparison, Germany has a relatively poor ranking. It is measured by the so-called TEA rate (Total early-stage entrepreneurial Activity), what expresses the percentage of individuals aged 18-64 who are either a nascent entrepreneur or owner-manager of a new business.[4] Among the innovation-based economies, Germany has a TEA rate of 5.27 percent (EU average 7.8 percent) while the United States has a TEA rate of 13.81

---

[1] Metzger und KfW Bankengruppe 2015, p. 2.
[2] BMWI Bundesministerium für Wirtschaft und Energie 2014
[3] Ripsas und Tröger 2014, p. 16.
[4] Singer et al. 2014, p. 24.

percent.[5] That shows at present Germany cannot be regarded as a founder country. However, in order to keep a leading position in the world economy Germany needs more entrepreneurs and therefore the federal government has to improve the framework conditions for entrepreneurs.

2 Existing Knowledge

The word entrepreneur has almost a mystical ring. For many persons, it triggers mental images of Silicon Valley technology startups like Facebook and Twitter along with vivid thoughts of the huge fame and vast wealth of these entrepreneurs. Similarly, most of the people interpret the term entrepreneurship as meaning what entrepreneurs do or mix it up with terms like management, leadership and foundation of an enterprise. That shows that many similar vague words coexist and makes it necessary to clearly distinguish the almost overlapping terms in order to avoid confusion.

2.1 Concept of Entrepreneurship

2.1.1 Derivation

The term entrepreneurship is derived from the Latin verb "prehendere" and can be roughly translated as "take action". In the French language exists a further reference with the verb "entreprendre".[6] According to Fallgartner in the 16th century in French by the term entrepreneur was meant a soldier of fortune. Since the 18th century the concept of the entrepreneur is attributed to the Irish Richard Cantillon. With the term he meant someone who runs a business and carries the risk of profit and loss by their own. Since then, the concept of the entrepreneur is closely linked to business practices.[7]

---

[5] Singer et al. 2014, p. 35.
[6] Freiling 2006, p. 11.
[7] Fallgatter 2002, p. 12.

2.1.2   Delimitation to other terms

In German, the term entrepreneurship is often translated as Unternehmertum. The authors Hering and Vincenti also use both terms as synonymous with the reason that a limitation of the term "entrepreneur" in the context of business foundation was unnecessary and would create confusion. They recommend using the term company founder in this context. The concept of businessman (Unternehmer) is aimed more to the ownership position and management functions of such persons while the term entrepreneur the innovative and dynamic element represents.[8] This is also the view of Peter F. Drucker.[9]

A closer examination of the concept of leadership and management shows that leadership and management are components of entrepreneurship. However, this is related to a specific context. Leadership is the proactive and creative basic orientation of entrepreneurship and sets out the framework to be completed by the management. Leadership relates to that area of entrepreneurship that recognizes business potentials, develops and promotes innovation and creates new visions. Management uses this preparatory work and refined this in example by formulating objectives and strategies. Also it is responsible for Implementation of the defined objectives. That makes clear leadership and management is an integrated unit that has to be matched.[10]

Finally, it is necessary to distinguish entrepreneurship to the terms business foundation and business administration. According to Nathusius the concept of business foundation describes a process in which an individual gets an occupational independence.[11] This autonomy implies that the relevant person is no longer bound to superior's instructions and their livelihood is based on income generation through economic activity.[12] Entrepreneurship includes the two cases and complements these, among other things by team foundations and corporate venturing. Corporate venturing means entrepreneurship in principle may also refer to salaried workers. In

---

[8] Hering und Aurelio J.F Vincenti 2005, p. 154ff.
[9] Drucker 1985, p. 24f.
[10] Hinterhuber 2004, p. 20.
[11] Nathusius 2003, p. 177.
[12] Hering und Aurelio J.F Vincenti 2005, p. 7.

addition, entrepreneurship can also be present if the activity is not fully used to secure the livelihood.[13]

2.1.3 Definition

Over time, the definition of entrepreneur and entrepreneurship has experienced an extensive transformation. For Knight the entrepreneur was primarily a carrier of uncertainty.[14] In contrast Schumpeters image of an entrepreneurs was marked by his innovative behavior and the concept of "creative destruction" of market balance.[15] Similarly is the view of Professor Faltin who became much attention for his bestseller "Brain versus Capital". Accordingly to the book, entrepreneurship is a dynamic process that does not invent anything, but rearranged and transferred existing conceptual business models into innovation. In this regard, Professor Faltin refers often to business foundations.[16] Nowadays Entrepreneurship refers to an exploiting of entrepreneurial opportunities as well as the creative entrepreneurial process in an organization.[17] Basically, it can be noted, in the literature no consistent understanding of the term entrepreneurship exists and some authors represent the opinion that entrepreneurship is not yet conclusively defined and it is generally difficult to define.[18] Often the term is linked to startups and small business foundations.

2.2 Concept of Startup

Most people using the term startup and small business foundation as synonymous but they have to be distinguished. Startup founder are entrepreneurs. They look for market gaps, develop new technologies, create new business models and optimize supply chains. In contrast the founders of small businesses often start out of necessity or because of lack of alternative sources of income.[19] However, science and practice have very different interpretations and definitions of the term startup. Most

---

[13] Freiling 2006, p. 24.
[14] Knight 2009
[15] Schumpeter 1952
[16] Faltin 2012
[17] Kollmann
[18] De 2005, p. 17.
[19] Ripsas und Tröger 2014, p. 4.

definitions say, that a startup has to be highly innovative related to their business model or technology. A similar definition uses the DSM (Deutscher Startup Monitor). In order to be considered as a startup a young company has to fulfill the first and at least one out of the two other following conditions.

- Startups are younger than 10 years.
- Startups are highly innovative with their technology and / or their business model.
- Startups who (seek at) a significant employee and / or revenue growth.[20]

2.3 Business foundations in Germany

In Germany starting a business is a relatively rare event. Indeed the startup activities since 2012 have again risen slightly after year of decreasing as the following chart demonstrates. However an international comparison of innovation-driven countries from 2014 shows Germany is rank at number 27 out of 29.[21]

Figure 1: Founder rates in Germany 2002-2014. Graphic is based on KfW-Gründungsmonitor 2015, p. 2.

A closer look at Figure 1 illustrates that the majority of business creation takes place in secondary occupation (57%). The bulk of these foundations (70%) occur in the service sector as Figure 2 shows. In 2014, with 34% the area of economic services

---

[20] Ripsas und Tröger 2014, p. 11.
[21] Sternberg et al. 2015, p. 9.

predominates followed by the personal services with 27%. A further 6% account for the field of other services that includes financial services, transport and communication. The trade (18%) and the manufacturing sector (15%) usually are balanced. A look at the start-up activity by fields of activity of the founders shows an interesting development: The number of founders in professional fields of activity has risen sharply, while the start-up activities in industry fields of activity subsided. This development can be observed for some time: The start-up activity is increasingly driven by entrepreneurs in professional fields of activity. This proportion has more than doubled over the past 10 years and is the reason for the slightly increase of startup activities. Table 1 shows the main professional activity fields.[22]

Figure 2: Foundations by sector.
Source: KfW-Gründungsmonitor 2015, p. 2.

Table 1: Top 10 startup projects in freelancer field.
Source: KfW-Gründungsmonitor 2015, p. 3.

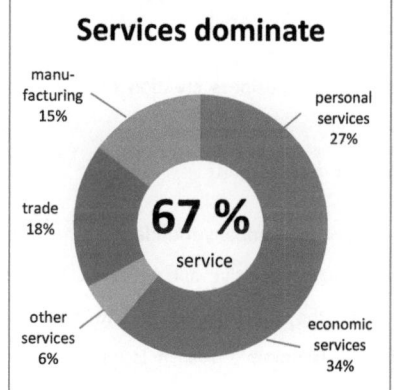

Ranking		Field of activity
2014	Δ2013	
1	●	Management consultancy
2	⬆	Dozentur
3	⬇	Child Day Care
4	⬆	Web design
5	●	Engineering office
6	⬆	Translations
7	⬆	Psychotherapy
8	⬆	Softwareengineering
9	⬆	Legal Consultancy
10	⬆	Coaching

Of the 915,000 people who started 2014 their own business, were 44% women. Thus, the proportion of women at the start-up activity is on a constant high level in the last 10 years. Most founders are between 25 and 35 years old, have successfully completed either a professional education (50%) or a university degree (31%) and mainly use own funds finance the start-up.[23]

---

[22] Metzger und KfW Bankengruppe 2015, p. 3.
[23] Metzger und KfW Bankengruppe 2015, p. 4 ff.

3   Research question and objectives

The preceding chapter presented the current body of knowledge concerning the topic of research. It turned out that an increasing proportion of business-creations take place in the service sector. A large part of them are software companies that developing applications for mobile devices. The growth forecast in the app market is still unbroken, since gadget like SmartWatch and smartphones have a constantly need for new application. Companies which design apps often use completely different business models as traditionally companies. Therefore, the requirements differ in terms of starting capital, legal form and the entire establishment process.

The objective of the proposed work is to work out how entrepreneurs nowadays can successful found a technology driven startup and how should this proceed. Therefore the following research questions should be answered:

- What steps are necessary for the business creation of a technology-driven company?
- Which features require the new organization?

The first question aims to find out how the company foundation at technology-driven companies can be proceed and managed effective and efficient. That means what steps are necessary, at what time they are necessary and how can they be implemented as quickly and cheaply as possible. Also it is interesting how can be reduced or avoided bureaucracy in the startup process.

The second question deals with the possibility if by using innovative new business models also new corporate structures can be used. This means is it possible to source out company parts like e.g. accountancy from the very beginning?

Another purpose of this study is to develop concrete action recommendations for company founders in technology-driven companies.

4 Structure and methodology

In order to structure the research activities it is mandatory to develop a systematic plan in order to study a scientific problem efficiently. Furthermore is it necessary to define the different research types that might be used to collect and analyze the needed data.

4.1 Data collection

The research questions defined in the preceding chapter are to be answered in the research paper. For this matter the research starts with a detailed overview on the current literature in order to get an idea how the entrepreneur process looks in general. Thus the factors which have a significant impact on the startup process will be defined and interpreted. Also these factors will be compared to each other and ranked by relevance. Furthermore the relationship between each single factor will be demonstrated. This is the basis to apply the findings to a technology-driven company in order to create a model process and to verify the assumed results.

Afterward a questionnaire will be created which is composed to verify the results of the literature review. The target group for the questionnaire is only entrepreneurs who have already started a business. This also integrates entrepreneurs who fault already with their business ideas. The questionnaire will include multiple choice and open questions which refer to the startup process and will consist of maximum 20 questions. The time to fill out should not be more than 10 minutes. The questionnaire should be handed out online to at least 100 entrepreneurs in order to get a reliable data base. Incorrectly or incompletely filled questionnaires are not considered in the evaluation. The aim of the questionnaire is to uncover constantly recurring difficulties in praxis within the business creation process. Also it should be demonstrated at which time the problems occur and why they occur. Thereby the significant factors which affect the startup process should be analyzed, evaluated and interpreted. This allows to show the discrepancies between theory and practice and to define a model for the startup process.

A further important resource for the qualitative data collection will be the interviews with people who started already a business. The focus will be at people who started a technology based startup. To generate a sufficient data base, at least five but not more than ten interviews are conducted. There are only carried out personal standardized interviews with the same open-ended questions are asked to all interviewees. This approach facilitates faster interviews and a more easily analysis and comparison.

The data collected by the procedure previously described may be regarded as not representative sampling due to the limited amount of data. However, this data base will be sufficient in order to be able to detect a rough direction as a pattern what the founding process might look like.

4.2   Timescale

The research described above will be likely conducted during the authors' fifth semester of the MBA (Master of Business Administration) program. This takes place from October 2015 to March 2016. Preparing works already started with the present proposal. The overall structure of the master thesis has to be refined with the tutor to begin of October 2015, in order to start writing and refining the literature review till mid-November 2015. Immediately after the refining activities of the research question and the methodical part of the thesis begins. Furthermore the questionnaire and the interviews are to be prepared and pre-tested by the test sample group. The data collection itself shall start at December and be finalized at mid-January. The evaluation of the questionnaires and interviews will then take place till mid-February. The final revision and edition of the thesis will be done in February, in order to submit the thesis in March 2016.

4.3   Resources

The financial effort is very much negligible as the books for the literature review can be borrowed free of charge at the library. Also the questionnaire can be created and send away without creating cost. During the interviews cost can occur for the arrival and departure. Also, these costs can be neglected due to the small amount.

References

Internet sources:

BMWI Bundesministerium für Wirtschaft und Energie (Hg.) (2014): Existenzgründung. Gründungsgeschehen - Zahlen, Daten, Fakten. Referat Öffentlichkeitsarbeit. Online verfügbar unter http://www.bmwi.de/DE/Themen/Mittelstand/Gruendungen-und-Unternehmensnachfolge/existenzgruendung.html, zuletzt aktualisiert am 14.11.2014, zuletzt geprüft am 05.06.2015.

Kollmann, Tobias: Entrepreneurship. Hg. v. Springer Gabler Verlag. Online verfügbar unter http://wirtschaftslexikon.gabler.de/Archiv/152051/entrepreneurship-v7.html.

Literature sources:

De, Dennis (2005): Entrepreneurship. Gründung und Wachstum von kleinen und mittleren Unternehmen. 1. Aufl. München, Boston [u.a.]: Pearson Studium (Wirtschaft).

Drucker, Peter F. (1985): Innovation and entrepreneurship. Practice and principles. London: Heinemann.

Fallgatter, Michael (2002): Theorie des Entrepreneurship. Perspektiven zur Erforschung der Entstehung und Entwicklung junger Unternehmungen. 1. Aufl. Wiesbaden: Dt. Univ.-Verl (Neue betriebswirtschaftliche Forschung, Bd. 299).

Faltin, Günter (2012): Kopf schlägt Kapital. Die ganz andere Art, ein Unternehmen zu gründen ; von der Lust, ein Entrepreneur zu sein. Ungekürzte Ausg. München: Dt. Taschenbuch-Verl (dtv, 34757).

Freiling, Jörg (2006): Entrepeneurship. Theoretische Grundlagen und unternehmerische Praxis. München: Franz Vahlen.

Hering, Thomas; Aurelio J.F Vincenti (2005): Unternehmensgründung. 1. Aufl. München: Oldenbourg.

Hinterhuber, H. H. (2004): Leadership. 3. Auflage. Frankfurt/M.

Knight, Frank H. (2009): Risk, uncertainty, and profit. New ed. Kissimmee, Fla: Signalman Publishing.

Metzger, Georg; KfW Bankengruppe (2015): KfW-Gründungsmonitor 2015. Gründungstätigkeit nimmt zu – Freiberufliche Tätigkeitsfelder dominieren. Frankfurt am Main: KfW Bankengruppe.

Nathusius, Klaus (2003): Finanzierungsinstrumente für unterschiedliche Gründungs-Modelle. Kassel: in. ZfbF, 55. Jg., S. 158-193.

Ripsas, Sven; Tröger, Steffen (2014): Deutscher Startup Monitor #DSM. Berlin: KPMG AG.

Schumpeter, Joseph A. (1952): Theorie der wirtschaftlichen Entwicklung. 5. Aufl.: Duncker & Humblot.

Singer, Salvica; Amoos, Jose, Ernesto; Moska, Daniel (2014): GEM Global Entrepreneurship Monitor 2014 Global Report. London: Global Entrepreneurship Research Association.

Sternberg, R.; Vorderwülbecke, A.; Brixy U. (2015): GEM Global Entrepreneurship Monitor. Unternehmensgründungen im weltweiten Vergleich. Länderbericht Deutschland 2014.